Make A List

Copyright © 2017 by Cori Nevruz
All rights reserved.
This book or any portion thereof may not be reproduced or used in any manner whatsoever without the express written permission of the author except for the use of brief quotations in a book review.

First Printing, 2017

When you're feeling overwhelmed
and need to get things done,

Take a moment,
MAKE A LIST,
then check them off
one-by-one.

My List

You have so many things to do
and don't want to forget.

See them on a piece of paper,
you'll get them done I bet!

You're heading to the grocery store and need supplies for dinner.

MAKE A LIST of the food you need, and you'll check out a winner!

GROCERY LIST

1. Eggs
2. MILK
3. Sauce (tomato)
4. Bacon
5. yogurt
6. fruit
7. vegetables
8. Bread

Summer Wish List:

- ☐ Pool Time
- ☑ Sleepovers
- ☐ Camps
- ☐ Go to the beach
- ☑ July Fourth
- ☐ Creating
- ☐ Reading
- ☑ Hang Out with Friends
- ☐ Go to the Movies
- ☑ Sports
- ☑ Birthday Parties
- ☐ Color and draw

Summer vacation is
around the corner,
there's so much fun in store!

MAKE A LIST of things to do
and you will get to more.

Your family wants to take a trip, vacation or car ride.

MAKE A LIST together,
it will help you all decide.

Family Vacations

- [x] Beach house
- [x] N.C. Zoo
- [ ] Disney World
- [ ] The Mountains

After school list

- [ ] Unpack backpack
- [ ] Do homework
- [ ] Read for 30 minutes
- [ ] Practice instrument
- [ ] Clean Room

Your mom gave you a
list of chores
to finish before you play.

Checking them off will
feel so good
that you will shout
HURRAY!

When you have some time
and you are not sure what to do,

MAKE A TOP TEN LIST
of your favorites to review.

Favorite Games

1. Chess
2. Codemaster
3. Ticket to Ride
4. Clue
5. Checkers
6. Magic
7. Chocolate Fix
8. Monopoly
9. Zingo
10. Bingo

Birthday List

1. battle masters
2. Ninjago lego sets
3. tree house
4. lego toy Pythore
5. ninja costume with a black belt

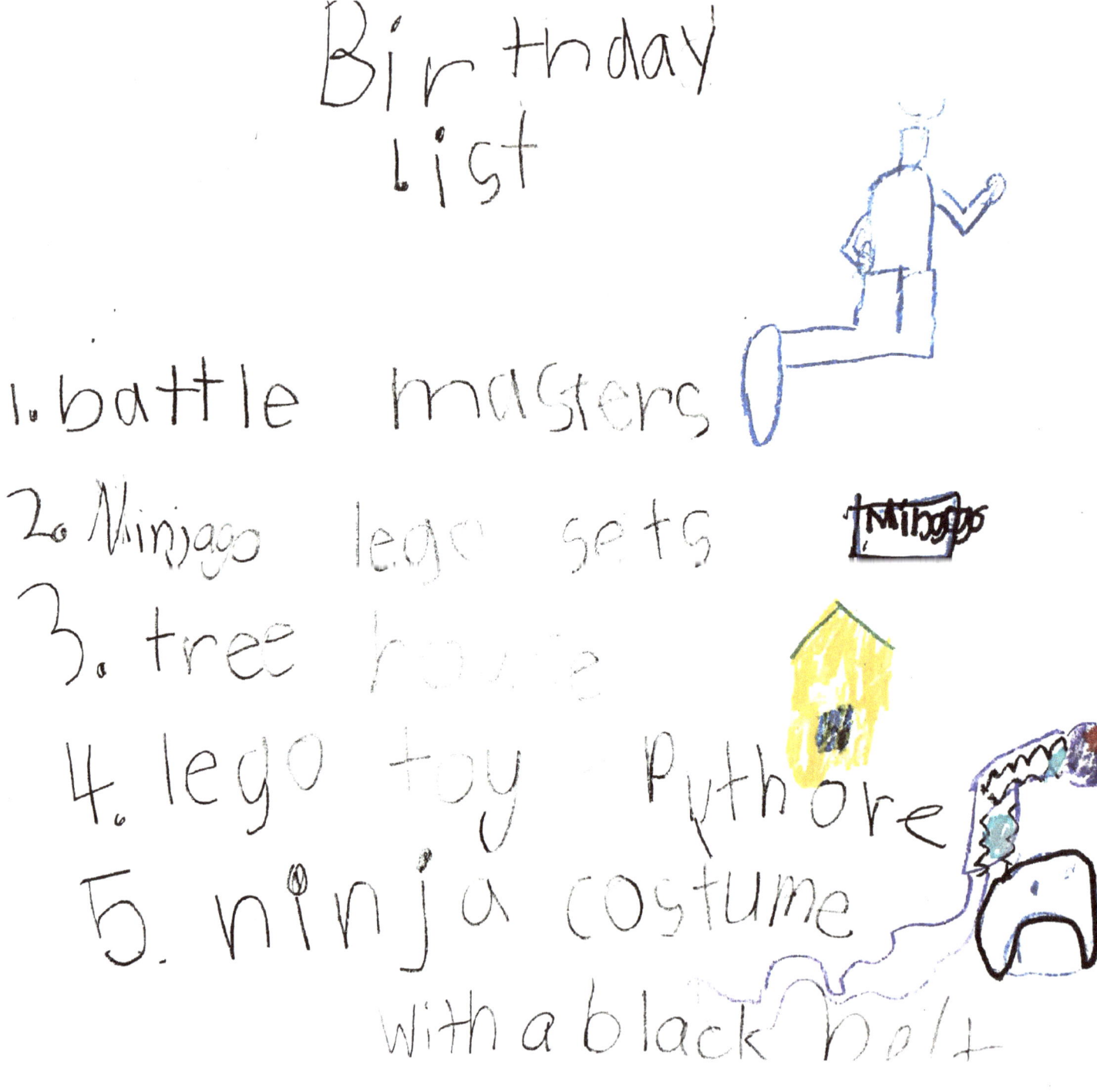

Your birthday is almost here
and you're not sure what to ask for.

MAKE A BIRTHDAY LIST
of toys from your favorite store.

Making lists is fun and quick,
try it and you'll see.

And when a check goes on your list,
so happy you will be!

MAKE A LIST

- ☐ Birthday List
- ☐ Christmas List
- ☐ Wish List
- ☐ To-do List
- ☐ Summer Bucket List
- ☐ Daily Chore List
- ☐ Grocery List
- ☐ Family Vacation List
- ☐ Dream Vacation List
- ☐ Top Ten List
    - ☐ Books
    - ☐ Games
    - ☐ Movies
    - ☐ Songs
    - ☐ Teams
    - ☐ Food
    - ☐ Cars
    - ☐ Toys

www.ingramcontent.com/pod-product-compliance
Lightning Source LLC
Chambersburg PA
CBHW061400160426

42811CB00099B/1358